Many Stars & More String Games

★ ★ ★ ★ ★ ★ ★ ★ ★ ★ ★ ★ ★ ★ ★ ★ ★ ★ ★ ★

by Camilla Gryski

Illustrated by Tom Sankey

William Morrow and Company
New York

Text copyright © 1985 by Camilla Gryski
Illustrations copyright © 1985 by Tom Sankey
Published in Canada by Kids Can Press, Toronto, Ontario.

1 2 3 4 5 6 7 8 9 10

Library of Congress Cataloging in Publication Data
Gryski, Camilla.   Many stars & more string games.
Sequel to: Cat's cradle, owl's eyes. Summary: More information on making string figures with step-by-step instructions for specific figures, games, and stories in string.   1. String figures—Juvenile literature.   [1. String figures.   2. Games] I. Sankey, Tom, ill.   II. Title.   GV1218.S8G78 1985   793′.9   85-4875
ISBN 0-688-05793-4 (lib. bdg.)
ISBN 0-688-05792-6 (pbk.)

This one is for Chester

I am indebted to the anthropologists who patiently learned, and painstakingly recorded, string figures and their traditions: Dr. A.C. Haddon, Kathleen Haddon, Caroline Furness Jayne, G. Landtman, James Hornell, Lyle Dickey, Diamond Jenness, Camilla Wedgwood, Honor Maude, and many others. Through their efforts, string figures have been preserved and can be learned and shared today.

My thanks to Honor Maude for her kind permission to use the story of **The Reluctant Sun**, recorded by Arthur Grimble and quoted in *String Figures from the Gilbert Islands*, The Polynesian Society, Wellington, New Zealand, 1958.

Table of Contents

All About String Figures

People often ask why I like string figures so much. There's a delight in having rabbits, birds, ghosts, and butterflies in my pockets, and knowing that my fingers can create them whenever I feel like it. The figures are often very intricate and beautiful, and the making of the figures and the flow of the finger movements are as satisfying as the end result.

String figures are also a fascinating part of history. They were collected by anthropologists who wanted to learn about the customs and cultures of the native peoples they studied. The first anthropologists brought back only drawings of string games, or sometimes the finished string patterns glued to pieces of card. These patterns were beautiful artifacts, but it wasn't until Alfred Haddon invented a language for string figures in the 1890s and began to teach them, that they came alive.

In the past, there was something secret and magical about string games. Sometimes they were used as passwords. Indians on Vancouver Island used the string figure "Threading a Closed Loop" to distinguish friends from enemies when they had meetings of their secret society. You and your friends can choose whichever figure you like best for your club!

In the South Pacific, string games carried their own secret messages. Someone might make a figure which said, "Let's go fishing,"or a figure that asked for support for a raid on an enemy village. And if an attack was expected, string figures helped everyone to stay awake.

In the Society Islands, string figures were called *Fai*, the same word that was used for the meshes of the sorcerer's net.

People could also play together as they made string figures. In Africa, one person would begin a string figure, someone else would say, "I will buy it from you," then take over and finish the figure. Try it — it's harder than it sounds!

Among the Maoris, two friends would agree on a figure, then sitting back to back, make it. Afterwards, they would compare the end results.

Today you can play string games in many different ways. You can have string figure races, or you and a friend can make one string figure together. One person uses only the right hand and one person uses only the left. Keep those other hands behind your backs, even though it's very tempting to use them to help out.

Some string games are designed for two people, like the game of Cat's Cradle, or the Ghost Dance which takes not only two people, but two strings as well.

In *Many Stars and More String Games* you'll also find a section about storytelling with string.

The figures in this book are arranged in order of difficulty. The easier figures, with fewer steps, are near the beginning. Learn them before you move on to the more difficult figures. Don't get discouraged. The more figures you do, the easier it will be to understand the language that tells you and your fingers what to do next.

Have fun with your string – and share string games with your friends!

About the String

The Inuit used sinew or a leather thong to make their string figures. Other peoples farther south made twine from the inside of bark. We are told that Tikopian children in the Pacific Islands area preferred fibre from the hibiscus tree, although they would use a length of fishing line if it was handy. Some people even used human hair, finely braided.

Fortunately, you don't have to go out into the woods or cut your hair to get a good string for making string figures.

You can use ordinary white butcher's string knotted together at the ends. Macrame cord also works quite well, as it is thicker than string. A thicker string loop will better show off your string figures.

Dressmaker's supply stores sell nylon cord, (usually by the metre or foot). This kind of cord is probably the best, and because it is woven, not plied or twisted, it won't crease. It can be joined without a knot. A knot in your string loop can cause tangles, and figures that move won't go smoothly if there is a knot in the way.

How to Make Your String

You need about two metres (six feet) of string or cord, so that your string loop will measure one metre (three feet) when it is joined. This is a standard size. If this length seems uncomfortably long, a shorter string is fine for most of the figures.

The string can be either tied or melted together.

To tie your string

You need a knot that won't slip, so a square knot is best.

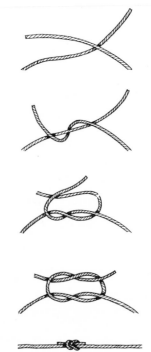

1. Lay the right end of the string across the left end.

2. Put this right end under the left string to tie the first part of the knot.

3. Lay the new left end across the new right end.

4. Put this new left end under the new right string and tighten the knot.

5. Trim the ends to make the knot neat.

To melt your string

If the cord is nylon or some other synthetic fibre, you can melt the ends together. Joining the string takes practice, and it has to be done quickly while the cord is hot. You will probably need some help, so please do this with an adult.

1. Hold the ends of the string near each other, about one to two centimetres (one-half an inch) above a candle flame. If the ends are not melting at all, they are too far away from the flame. They will singe if you are holding them too close.

2. When the ends are gooey, stick them together.

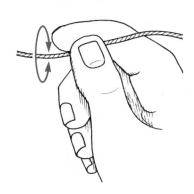

3. Count to five to let them cool, then roll them between your fingers to smooth the join.

You have now made your "play string" or "ayahaak" as the Inuit call it.

Terminology
There's a Special Language

A long time ago, people made lists of the names of string figures, or brought back drawings of the finished patterns. Some even kept the string pattern itself, fastened to a piece of paper.

But once a string figure is finished, it is almost impossible to tell just how it was made. We can learn and teach each other string figures today because, in 1898, two anthropologists, Dr. A.C. Haddon and Dr. W.H.R. Rivers, invented a special language to describe the way string figures are made. Haddon and Rivers developed their special language to record all the steps it took to make the string figures they learned in the Torres Straits. Then, other anthropologists used this same language, or a simpler version of it, when they wanted to remember the string figures they saw in their travels.

The language used in this book to describe the making of the figures is similar to that used by Haddon and Rivers. The loops and the strings have names, and there are also names for some of the basic positions and moves.

About Loops

When the string goes around your finger or thumb, it makes a **loop.**

The loops take their names from their location on your hands: **thumb loop, index loop, middle finger loop, ring finger loop, little finger loop.**

If you move a loop from one finger to another, it gets a new name: a loop that was on your thumb but is now on your little finger is a new little finger loop.

Each loop has a **near string** — the one nearer (or closer) to you — and a **far string** — the one farther from you.

If there are two loops on your thumb or finger, one is the **lower loop** — the one near the base of your thumb or finger — and the other is the **upper loop** — the one near the top of your thumb or finger. Don't get these loops mixed up, and be sure to keep them apart.

About Making the Figures

As you make the figures in this book, you will be weaving the strings of the loops on your fingers. Your fingers or thumbs can go over or under the strings to pick up one or more strings, then go back to the basic position.

Sometimes you may **drop** or **release** a loop from your fingers.

It takes a little while to get used to holding your hands so that the strings don't drop off your fingers. If you accidentally drop a loop or a string, it is best to start all over again.

Now go and get your string — let's begin!

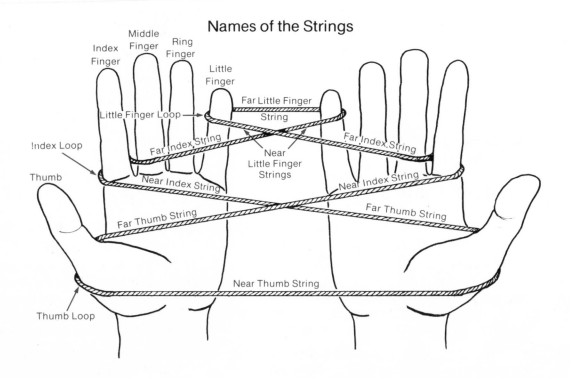

Names of the Strings

The Basic Position

Your hands begin in the **basic position** for most string figures and usually return to the basic position after each move.

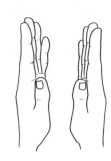

1. Your hands are parallel, the palms are facing each other, and your fingers are pointing up.

The hands in some of the pictures are not in the basic position. The hands are shown with the palms facing you so that you can see all the strings clearly.

Position 1

1. With your hands in the basic position, hang the loop of string on your thumbs. Stretch your hands as far apart as you can to make the string loop tight.

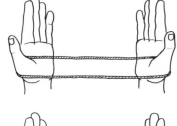

2. Pick up the far thumb string with your little fingers. The string that goes across the palm of your hand is called the **palmar string.**

Opening A

Many string figures begin with **Opening A.**

1. Put the string loop on your fingers in Position 1.

2. With your right index finger, pick up from below the palmar string on your left hand, and return to the basic position pulling this string on the back of your index finger as far as it will go.

3. With your left index finger, pick up the right palmar string, from below, in between the strings of the loop that goes around your right index finger. Return to the basic position, again pulling out the palmar string as far as it will go.

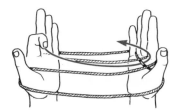
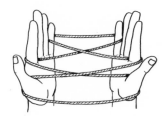

To Navaho a Loop

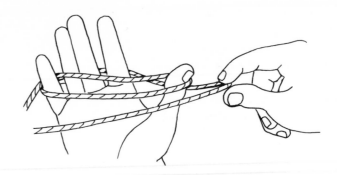

When you have two loops on your thumb or finger, a lower loop and an upper loop, you **Navaho** these loops by lifting the lower loop — with the thumb and index finger of your opposite hand, or with your teeth — up over the upper loop and over the tip of your finger or thumb.

You can also Navaho a loop by tipping down your thumb or finger, letting the lower loop slip off, then straightening up your thumb or finger again.

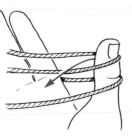 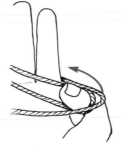 

To Share a Loop

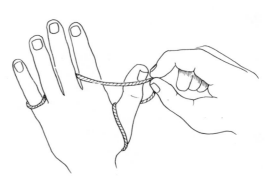

Sometimes you will **share a loop** between two fingers or a finger and your thumb. You use your opposite index finger and thumb to pull out the loop so that the other finger or thumb will fit into the loop as well.

To Extend a Figure

Sometimes the strings may be woven and a figure may be finished, but it needs to be **extended** by pulling the hands apart, or by turning or twisting the hands in a certain way. Extending the figure makes a tangle of strings magically turn into a beautiful pattern.

To Take the Figure Apart

Always take the figures apart gently, as tugging creates knots. If the figure has top and bottom straight strings which frame the pattern, pull these apart and the pattern will dissolve.

Getting a String or Strings

When the instructions tell you to **get** a string or strings, your finger or thumb goes under that string, picks up that string on its back (the back of your finger or thumb is the side with the fingernail), then returns to the basic position carrying the string with it. The instructions will tell you if you are to use your fingers or thumb to pick up the strings in a different way.

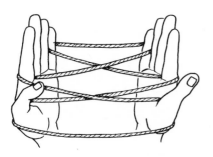 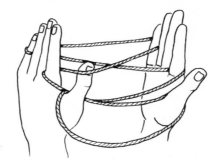 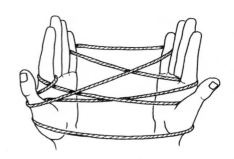

How to Double a String

For some figures, you can use a short string loop, or you can double your long string.

1. Hang the string loop over the fingers, but not the thumb, of your hand.

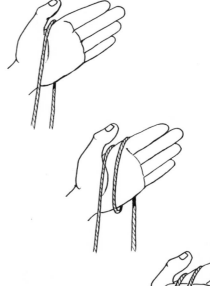

2. Wrap the back string of the hanging loop once around your hand.

3. Take hold of everything that crosses the palm of your hand (the loop and one hanging string) and pull these strings out as far as they will go.

The Moth or Spectacles

This is a Zulu string figure from Africa. When you've made the figure, you can put it up to your eyes as spectacles or glasses. It's also called the Moth.

Use a short string or double your long string loop for this figure.

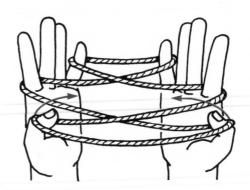

1. Do Opening A.

2. Your thumbs drop their loops.

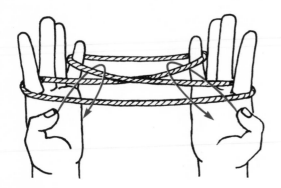

3. Your thumbs go over the strings of the index loops to get the near little finger strings and return.

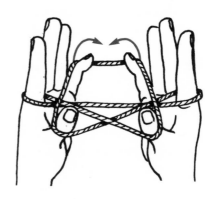

4. Your little fingers drop their loops.

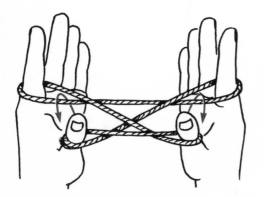

5. Your thumbs go up into the index loops and return with the near index strings.

6. Use your teeth or fingers to Navaho the thumb loops. (See page 10 for instructions on how to Navaho a loop.)

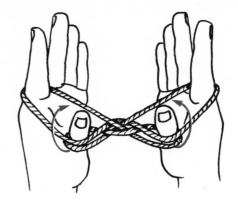

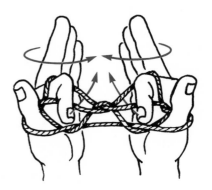

7. Hook your index fingers over the Navahoed loops which now cross in the centre of the figure and down into the index loops.

8. Turn your hands so that the palms face away from you and straighten up your index fingers to make the Moth. Don't worry about the index loops; they will slip off by themselves.

Don't pull the figure too tight. Make it tall rather than wide as you extend it.

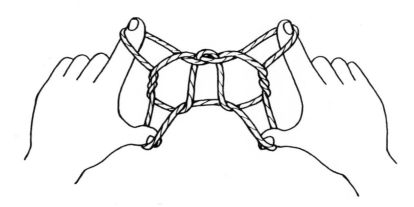

A String Trick

This one is from the Bantu people of Africa. It's not difficult, but it never fails to delight. Speed and smoothness add to the magical effect. And don't forget to clap!

1. Put the string loop around your neck, just below your ears and level with your mouth. Hold the side strings near the top of the loop so that you can cross them over easily.

2. Cross the strings over each other and, where they cross, bite them with your teeth. Be sure to cross your arms as you cross the strings; don't change hands as you cross them over. And don't let go of the strings!

3. Now uncross the strings by uncrossing your arms and hide the uncrossed strings with your lips.

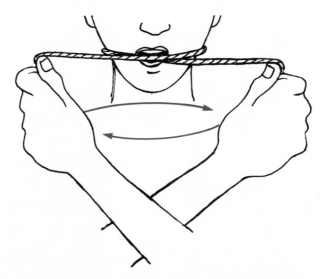

4. Put the long string loop right over your head. Your hands are still holding the ends of this loop.

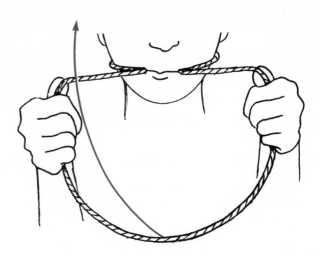

5. Clap your hands (and these strings) together — this is important.

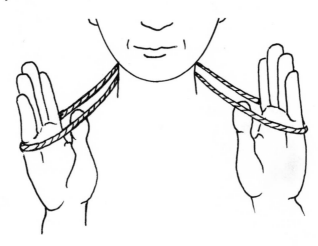

6. Release the strings in your mouth and stretch out your arms to show that the string loop is now at the back of your neck.

The Camp Bed

This figure came from central Africa where it was called The White Man's Camp Bed, but it might have been given a new name because its real one, The Breastplate the Fetish Man Wears, had magical significance. If you make it very wide, it's also Sumbo, a fishing net. Try wearing it as a necklace!

1. Double the string loop and hang it around your neck.

2. Put your left thumb into the double string loop from behind and hold the two strings of the loop on your thumb. Keep these strings apart — one near the base of your thumb, and one near the tip of your thumb.

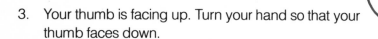

3. Your thumb is facing up. Turn your hand so that your thumb faces down.

4. Your right hand goes down into the space framed by your left arm and the strings, and your right thumb and index finger take the loop off the tip of your left thumb.

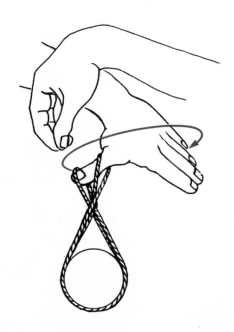

5. Bring this loop back out through the space, turn your hand so that your thumb faces up again, and put this loop on your left little finger. As you bring this loop out, make sure that you turn it over.

6. Your right thumb and index finger go through the little finger loop to get the far thumb string. Bring this string out through the strings of the little finger loop.

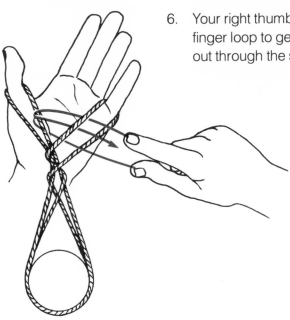

7. Your left little finger drops its loop.

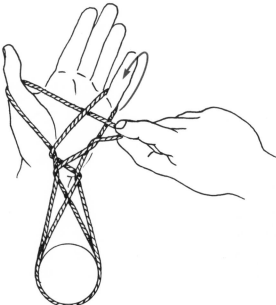

8. Put the loop held by your right index finger and thumb onto your left little finger.

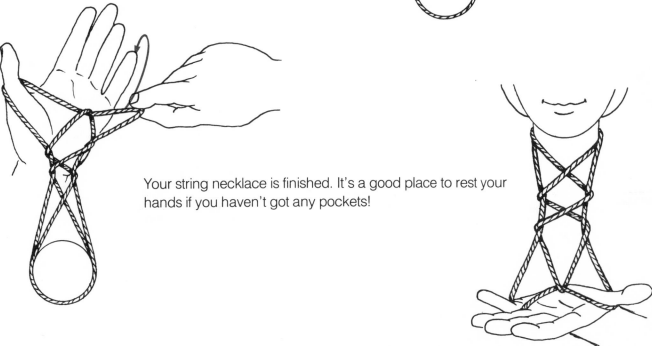

Your string necklace is finished. It's a good place to rest your hands if you haven't got any pockets!

Lairo or the Land Crab

This trick, or catch, originated in Fiji. The see sawing of the strings, the chanting, and especially the tap on the back of the hand are important parts of the magic!

1. Do Position 1, but with a cross in the string loop. To do this, you can lay the string loop down, make an X in it, then pick it up in Position 1.

2. Now do Opening A.

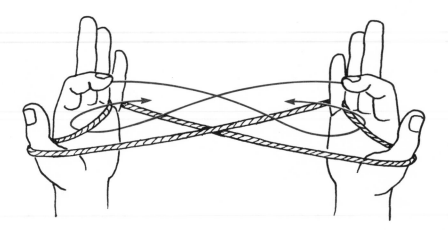

3. When you look down into the index loops, you can see an X. Go through the index loops, grab the X with your teeth, and bring it out through the index loops.

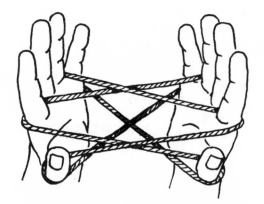

4. Ask a friend to put his/her hand into the triangular space framed by the strings you have in your mouth and the thumb strings.

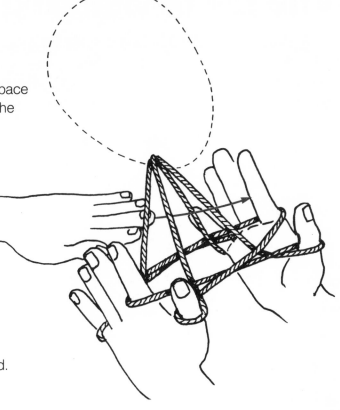

5. Release the mouth strings to trap your friend's hand.

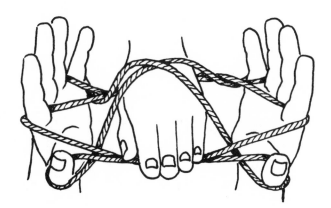

6. See saw your strings back and forth chanting:
   Land crab, land crab, will you bite or not?
   Your friend answers:
   I will bite.
   You ask:
   Whom will you bite, hairy tooth?
   Your friend replies:
   Get up and you and I will fly away.

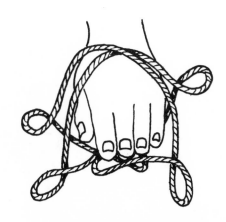

You then release all your loops and gently tap the back of your friend's hand. With a flourish, you pick up the strings lying across your friend's wrist and your friend is free.

The Eel or Catching Crabs

This string trick works in two different ways. It's also a good string picture of an eel. In Papua, it was an eel to be caught by the second player, but in the Gilbert Islands, the second player became the crab, caught when his/her fingers were trapped by the strings.

1. Hang the string loop on your little fingers.

2. Your right thumb goes down over both strings of the right little finger loop, then straightens up and returns carrying these strings with it. These strings are now thumb loops.

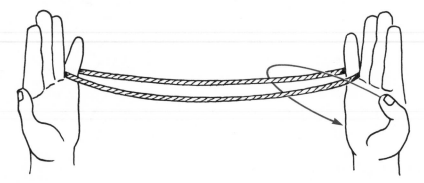

3. Your left thumb goes up under both right palmar strings and returns carrying these strings on its back.

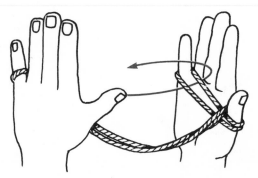

4. Your thumbs get both strings of the little finger loops and return.

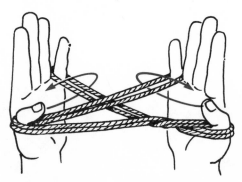

5. Your index fingers tip down and go up into the thumb loops to get the double far thumb strings and return.

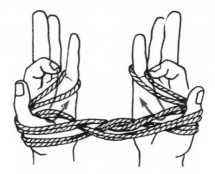

6. Extend the eel by moving your right hand up and tipping it so that the palm faces you, and by moving your left hand down and tipping it so that the palm also faces you. Now you can see the eel twined around the strings.

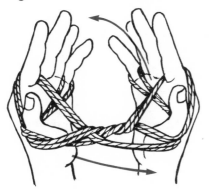

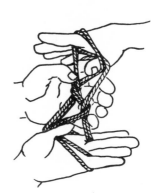

7. Ask someone to catch the eel by putting his/her hand around it. When you release the loops from your index fingers and thumbs and pull out the little finger loops, the eel slithers away. Of course, if your friend is holding onto the strings very tightly, both you and the eel are trapped!

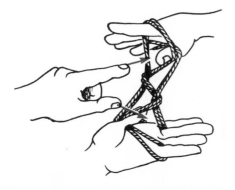

Now, to catch the crab, ask someone to put his/her middle finger into the shared right index/thumb loop, and his/her thumb into the shared left index/thumb loop. This time, when you release your index fingers and thumbs and pull out the little finger loops, you've caught your crab!

Open the Gate

In Hawaii, this figure is called Open the Gate. In Fiji, it shows a point of land and an island which are sadly separated, even when the tide goes out. And in New Guinea, two birds fly away from each other calling "Kokoko."

1. Do Opening A.

2. Your thumbs go over the strings of the index loops to get the near little finger strings and return.

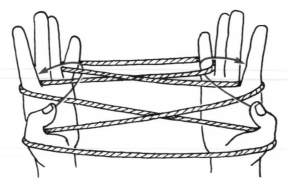

3. Your little fingers, without losing their loops, go over the strings of the index loops to get the far thumb strings and return.

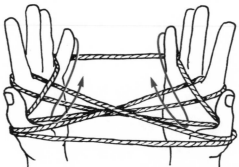

4. Your index fingers hook over the double palmar strings and go down into the index loops. Hold these palmar strings tightly under your index fingers to keep the strings steady.

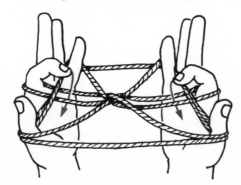

5. Your little fingers drop their loops.

6. Your thumbs drop their loops.

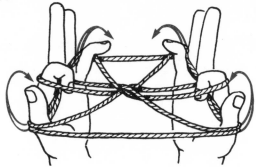

7. Still holding on tightly with your index fingers, let the old index loops slide off your index fingers. Don't pull your hands apart to let the palmar strings slide yet.

8. Put your middle, ring, and little fingers into the index loops.

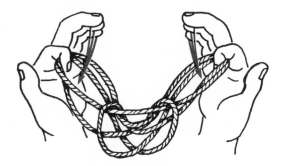

9. Now make the gate taller by using your thumbs to lift up the top strings of the loops held by your fingers.

10. As you pull your hands apart and let the double strings around your thumbs and under your fingers slide, the gate will open.

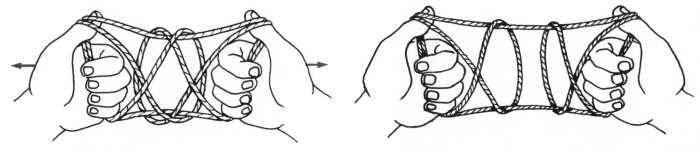

The Japanese Butterfly

There are many Japanese string figures of dragonflies and butterflies. String artist Bill Russell learned this one from a Japanese-Canadian schoolgirl. It's not too hard, and it's very beautiful.

1. Hang the string loop on your thumbs.

2. Your left little finger picks up, from below, the left far thumb string to put the string loop in Position 1 on your left hand.

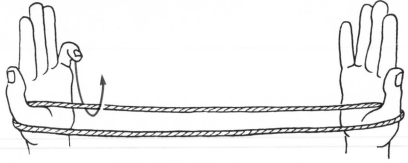

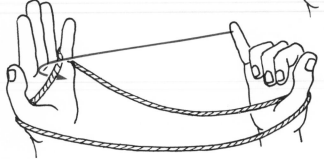

3. Bend down your right index, middle, and ring fingers, but leave your little finger standing tall to make the next move easier. Now your right little finger dives, from the top, down behind the left palmar string.

4. Turn your right little finger away from you and up, and return all your fingers to the basic position.

Both thumbs and little fingers have loops on them, and there is a cross in the middle of the figure. Make sure that the near little finger string is one straight string running from hand to hand.

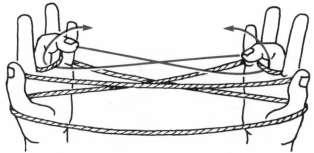

5. Your index fingers tip down and go up into the little finger loops to get the near little finger string and return.

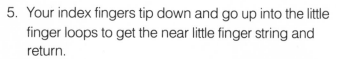

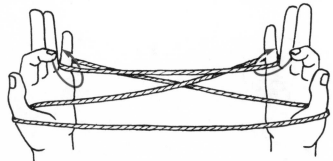

6. Now do Opening A with your middle fingers, picking up the loops that cross in front of your middle and ring fingers.

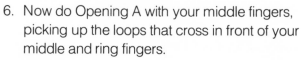

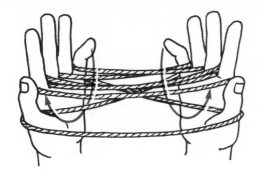

7. Turn your hands so that the palms are facing you. Your little fingers move over the strings to get the far thumb strings. Return your hands to the basic position.

8. Your index fingers hook over the palmar strings (the strings that run across the loops from thumbs to little fingers) and down into the index loops.

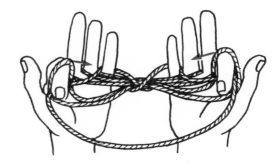

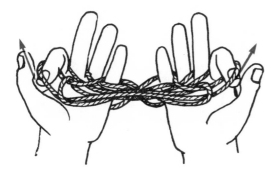

9. Your index fingers still hang on to these palmar strings while your thumbs release their loops.

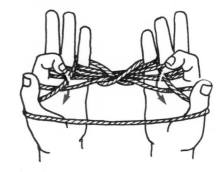

10. Now turn your hands again so that the palms are facing you, and let the old index loops slide off your index fingers.

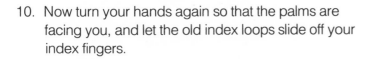

11. Your index fingers straighten up. The strings under your index fingers become the new index loops.

12. Return your hands to the basic position. Now turn your hands so that your fingers are pointing away from you to show off the Butterfly.

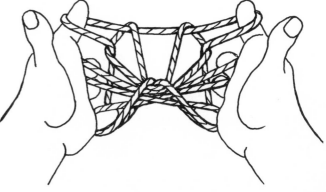

Fire

There are so many stories about heroes who stole fire from the gods that it's not surprising to find fire represented in string. Perhaps this figure shows the crossed sticks from the fire tree that smoked when they were rubbed together. In New Guinea, this figure was used to trick an unsuspecting friend. Its African name is Chellaba, or Turn Over, because of the way you turn over the strings to make the diamonds appear.

Double your long string or use a short string loop for this figure.

1. Do Position 1.

2. Your right thumb goes, from the top, down behind the left palmar string. Turn your thumb up towards you, bringing the palmar string with it, and return your hands to the basic position.

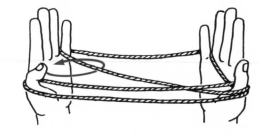

3. Your left thumb gets the left near little finger string and returns.

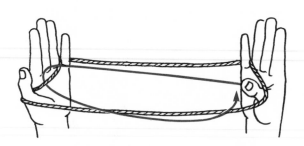

4. Your index fingers tip down and go up into the thumb loops to get the far thumb strings and return.

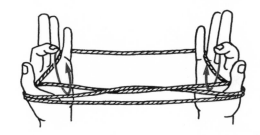

5. Navaho the thumb loops.

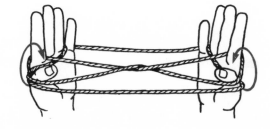

6. Your little fingers drop their loops.

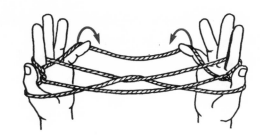

7. Now for that "turn over" extension.

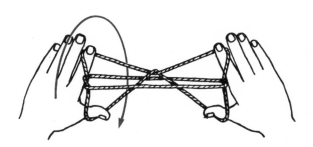

   a) Turn your hands so that both palms are facing down.

   b) Turn your left hand so that your fingers are pointing towards the right.

   c) Flip your left hand over so that the palm is facing up. As you do this, your fingers must go under the strings of the figure.

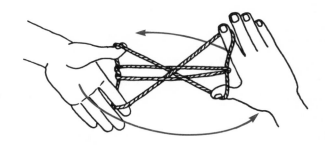

   d) Move your left hand, palm up, fingers first, over to the right. Your hand will cross over your right wrist.

   e) Now your left thumb is pointing up, and your left palm is facing out. Tip your right hand so that its thumb is also pointing up and its palm is also facing out.

   (Did you get it? Congratulations. It's a tricky move!)

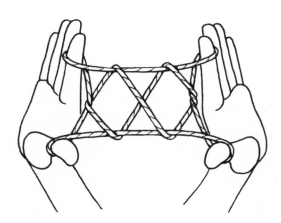

8. Here's how you trick your friend. Ask someone to blow the fire. To do this, your friend must bring his/her face close to your thumb and index finger. Now you can pinch a nose or mouth!

The Giant Clam

The Giant Clam comes from Fiji in the South Pacific. It opens and shuts when you seesaw your hands back and forth. This is one string figure that you can use as a kind of puppet.

1. Do Opening A.

2. Your thumbs drop their loops. Pull the strings out until they are tight.

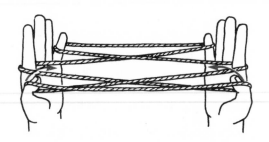

3. Your right thumb goes over and holds down, the strings of the right index loop and the right near little finger string. Turn your palm away from you and point your thumb down to make this move easier.

4. Your right index finger hooks down over the right far little finger string. Now your right thumb can release the strings it was holding down. As you straighten up your index finger, turn the palm of your right hand towards you so that the far little finger string can curve around the back of your index finger to become a new right upper index loop. Keep these index loops separate, the upper loop high on your index finger.

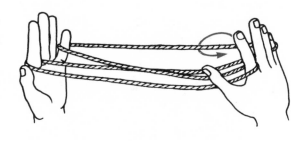

5. Your left index finger goes, from below, up into this new upper right index loop and pulls it out as you return your hands to the basic position. This loop is now shared between the index fingers.

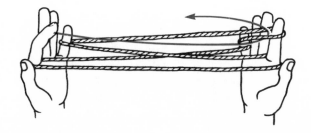

6. Your thumbs go under the strings of both sets of index loops to get the near little finger strings. Return under the strings of the index loops.

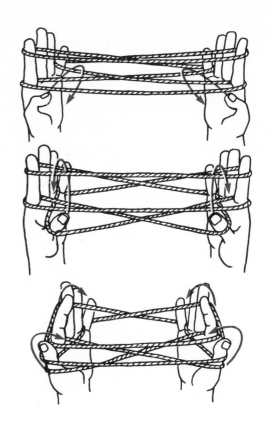

7. Your thumbs now go up into the upper index loops to share them.

8. Navaho the thumb loops with your fingers or your teeth, then let the upper index loops slip off your index fingers. Be sure to keep the lower index loops.

9. This is the Giant Clam. You can make it open and close and carry on conversations by seesawing your hands sideways so that first your thumbs, then your little fingers come close together.

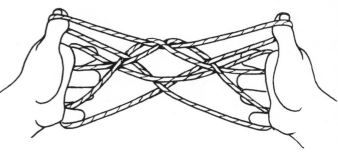

10. When you drop the loops from your little fingers and gently even out the loops on your thumbs and index fingers, you get a pattern which was called the Moon in Africa and the Mouth by the Maoris of New Zealand. Now read on for a strange story about an ancient use for it.

About 400 A.D., a Greek physician named Oribasius wrote a medical treatise. In it, he described how to make a special string sling. You can try making the same sling yourself with a long loop of string.

Make the Moon. Rest your chin in the central diamond of the figure and tie the four long loops up on top of your head. Your dislocated jaw is now in traction!

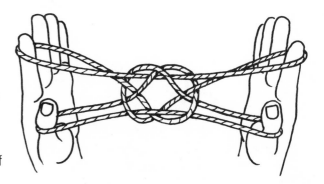

The Leashing of Lochiel's Dogs

This figure was collected in Scotland, but it's found in many other parts of the world and has many names: Ptarmigan's Feet, or Crow's Feet, in North America; Chicken Toes, or the Wooden Spoon, in Africa; and the Spade in New Zealand. It's a type of catch where strings are caught part way down the figure when loops are dropped.

1. Do Opening A.

2. Turn your hands so that the palms are facing you and put all your fingers down into the thumb loops.

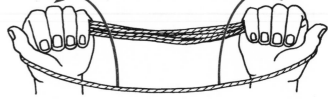

3. Throw the thumb loops over the backs of your hands and return your hands to the basic position. The loops around the backs of your hands should be lower than the index and little finger loops.

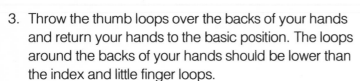

4. To transfer the index loops to your thumbs, your thumbs go up into the index loops. Now take your index fingers out of their loops.

5. Your right index finger and thumb lift the loop off the back of your left hand and put it on your left middle finger.

6. Your left index finger and thumb lift the loop off the back of your right hand and put it on your right middle finger.

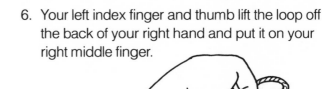

7. Your little fingers hook down over the far middle finger string and move it out of the way into the middle of the little finger loops. Now your little fingers can go down into the little finger loops to get the near little finger strings and straighten up.

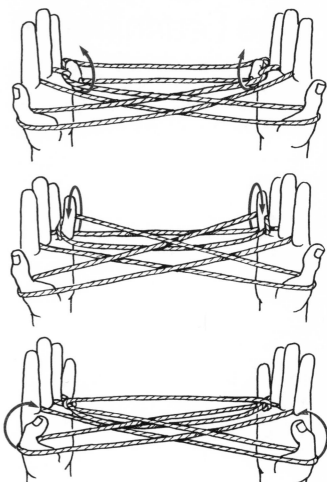

8. Each little finger now has two loops. To Navaho these loops, your right index finger and thumb pick up the lower far little finger string near your left little finger, carry it over the top of your left little finger, and let it lie on the near side of your little finger.

   Your left index finger and thumb pick up the lower far little finger string near your right little finger, carry it over the top of your right little finger, and let it lie on the near side of your right little finger. Return your hands to the basic position.

   The loops that you've Navahoed make one straight string which runs across the figure.

9. Your thumbs drop their loops. Now pull the strings until they are tight to make the dogs on their leashes.

10. To make Crow's Feet, you pick up the double strings in the middle of the figure with your teeth, and you bring your hands close together, palms up.

   Cameron of Lochiel was a seventeenth-century Scottish Highland chieftain who was famous for his feats of strength and his fierceness in battle.

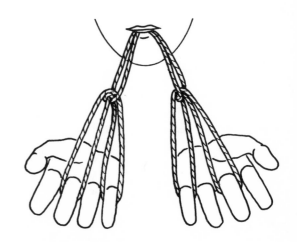

The Ghost Dance

It takes two people and two strings to make this dancing ghost from New Guinea. You can make it grow skinny or fat, hop, jump, or dance on one leg. The fun can go on until someone stamps on the floor and shouts to frighten the ghost which then collapses into a pile of loose strings.

Are you ready? The people are named A and B; the strings are numbered 1 and 2.

1. A and B hang string loop 1 around their necks. They sit or stand far enough apart so that the strings of the loop are tight.

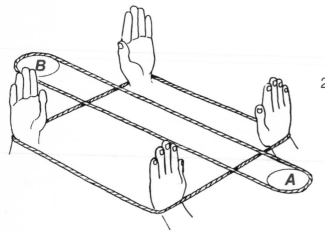

2. A and B put their hands, from below, up into string loop 2. The loop lies over their wrists. They bend their wrists so that their fingers are pointing up and their palms are facing away from them. String loop 2 now has wrist strings and side strings and is roughly square.

3. A's left index finger and thumb tip down to pick up A's left side string. A's right index finger and thumb tip down to pick up A's right side string.

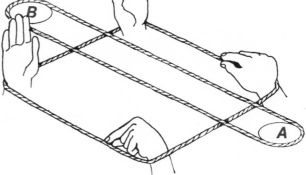

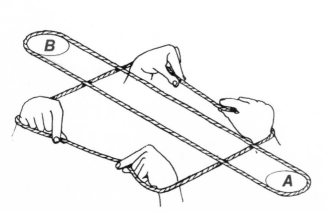

4. B does the same, so B's left index finger and thumb take B's left side string, and B's right index finger and thumb take B's right side string.

5. A's left and right hand want to exchange strings. So do B's. Be careful to keep the wrist loops as you do this. A's left hand and B's right hand, carrying their string, move towards the centre of the figure to meet A's right hand and B's left hand carrying their string. One side string will cross over, one under the other as the strings change hands.

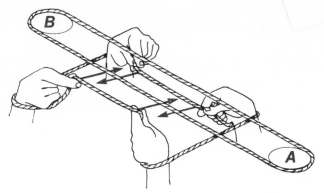

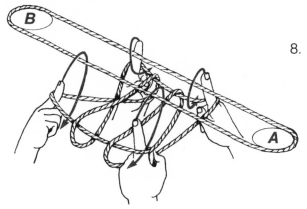

6. Now A and B let the wrist loops slide off their wrists and off their hands to lie over the crossed strings of loop 2.

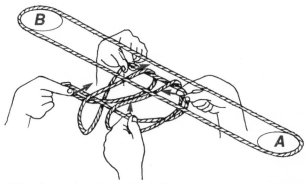

7. A and B are each holding two loops with their thumbs and index fingers. These loops now become index loops as A and B put their index fingers only up into them from below.

8. A and B raise string loop 2 until it rests just below string loop 1. Their index fingers hook down over string loop 1 and pull string loop 1 out through the old index loops. Don't worry about the old index loops — they will just slip off your index fingers.

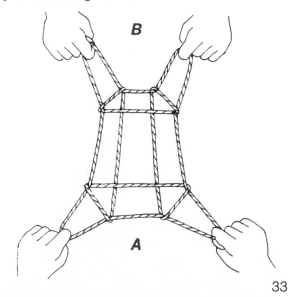

9. A and B take their heads out of string loop 1 and pull gently on the loops they are holding. You've made the ghost! Put the ghost's feet on the ground, make it stand up straight, and the ghost is ready to dance.

To make the ghost short and fat, A and B pull their hands apart. To make it tall and skinny, they bring their hands close together. Remember to keep the strings extended all the time. Now have fun making ghost noises — until someone shouts "Boo!"

Two Brown Bears and Their Caves

This Inuit string figure gives you two string pictures — one of the caves where the bears are sleeping and, when you release your index loops, one of the bears coming out of their caves and walking away in opposite directions. Can you tell a story to go with it?

1. Do Opening A.

2. Turn your hands so that the palms are facing you and put all your fingers down into the thumb loops.

3. Throw the thumb loops over the backs of your hands and return your hands to the basic position. Be sure to keep all the loops separate. The loops around the backs of your hands should be lower than the index loops and the little finger loops. Keep the index loops high up on your index fingers.

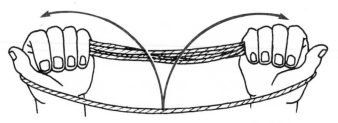

4. Your thumbs hook down the strings that go around the backs of your hands (the near strings of the hand loops), and go under the other strings to get the far little finger string. Return to the basic position bringing this string back out between the near index strings and the near strings of the hand loops.

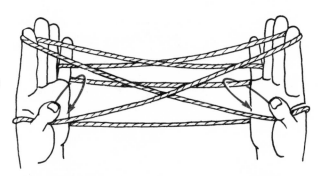

5. With your right thumb and index finger, take hold of the left thumb loop. Now take your left thumb out of its loop and put it back into its loop from the top.

6. With your left thumb and index finger, take hold of the right thumb loop. Now take your right thumb out of its loop and put it back into its loop from the top.

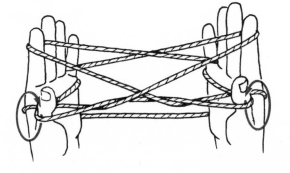

7. Turn your hands away from you, palms facing out and thumbs facing down. You have an upside down cave on each thumb. Make sure that the far string of the hand loops runs across these caves.

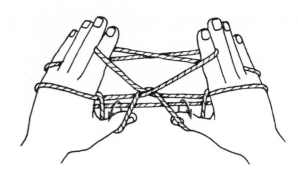

8. Your thumbs get the far string of the hand loops and bring it back out through the old thumb loops (the caves).

9. With your right thumb and index finger, take hold of the string that goes around the back of your left hand and lift it up over your fingers, but not over your thumb, to lie on the palm side of your left hand.

10. With your left thumb and index finger, take hold of the string that goes around the back of your right hand and lift it up over your fingers, but not your thumb, to lie on the palm side of your right hand. Now when you point your fingers away from you, you can see the two caves below the mountain.

11. When you release the loops from your index fingers and pull your hands gently apart, you can see the two bears coming out of their caves, each bear represented by a head and a body that curves around the string.

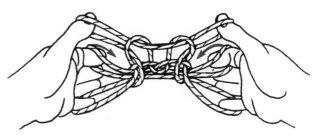

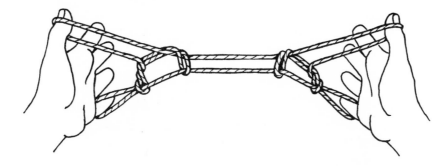

This figure is a variation of the Siberian House from *Cat's Cradle, Owl's Eyes,* so if the movements seemed familiar to you, they were!

The Well

This figure was found throughout the South Pacific and has many different names. In Fiji it was called Velovelo, the dugout canoe. The Murray Islanders called it Ti Meta, the nest of the Ti bird. It was also a basket or wooden food bowl. When you've made the Well, you can go on to make the Fence Around the Well.

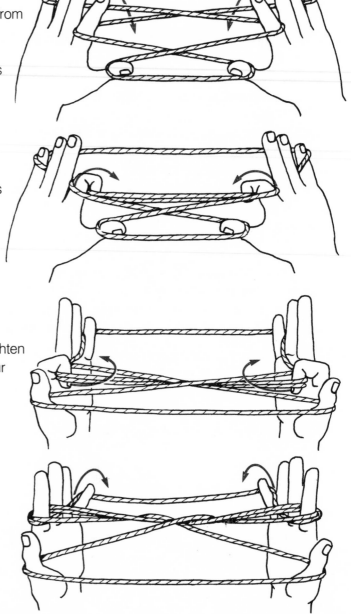

1. Do Opening A.

2. Turn your hands so that the palms are facing away from you.

3. Your index fingers go down into the little finger loops and hook down over the near little finger strings.

4. Let the index loops slide down on your index fingers until they are also held in the hooks of your index fingers.

5. Rotate your index fingers towards you as you straighten them up to return to the basic position. Don't let your index fingers get tangled in the thumb loops.

6. Your little fingers drop their loops.

   Each index finger now has two loops and there are loops on your thumbs.

7. Your middle, ring, and little fingers go down into the index loops from above, and hook down the far strings of the double index loops.

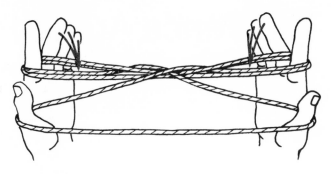

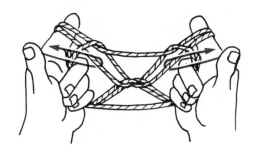

8. Now your middle, ring, and little fingers go up into the thumb loops from below, and hook down the straight near thumb string.

9. Your thumbs drop their loops. Turn your hands so that your index fingers are pointing away from you.

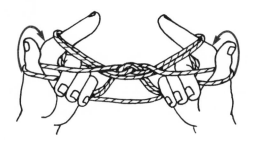

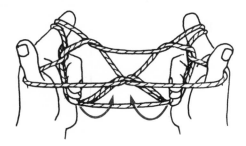

10. Find the strings that run down diagonally from your index fingers to the bottom of the figure. Your thumbs go in behind these strings and pull them forward on their backs as your thumbs return to the basic position.

11. Your middle, ring, and little fingers are holding down the double far strings of the index loops and the straight string of the old thumb loops. They release this straight string, but continue to hold down the far index strings. This is the Well.

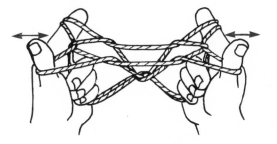

You can make the well deeper by bringing your thumbs closer together. When you pull your thumbs farther apart, you make the shallow, or dry, well.

Don't drop this figure if you want to go on to the Fence Around the Well on the next page.

The Fence Around the Well

The Fence Around the Well is a continuation of the Well. It's really very pretty.

1. Make the Well.

2. Your thumbs go up behind the double near index strings and return.

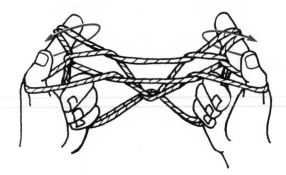

3. Navaho the thumb loops. To do this, use your fingers or teeth to move the lower thumb loops up over the two upper thumb loops and over the tops of your thumbs.

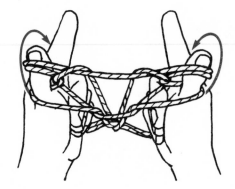

4. Your middle, ring, and little fingers release the loops they are holding down.

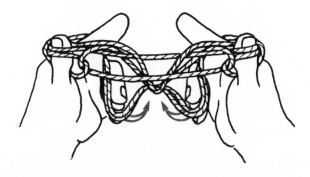

5. Your index fingers drop their loops.

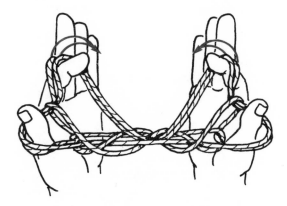

6. Now put all your fingers, from the top, down into the thumb loops to widen them and extend the Fence.

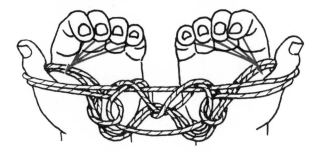

7. Turn your hands so that the thumbs are pointing up. Now the Fence is standing upright.

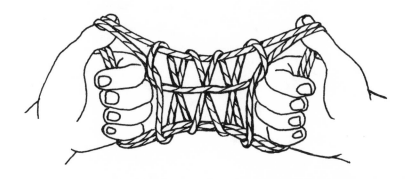

Maui's Lasso

This figure comes from Hawaii. It illustrates the well-known story of Maui's efforts to slow down the sun so that his mother would have time to do all her housework. You can turn to "Stories in String" to find out exactly how he did it!

1. Do Opening A.

2. Turn your hands so that the palms are facing away from you.

3. Your index fingers go down into the little finger loops and hook down over the near little finger strings.

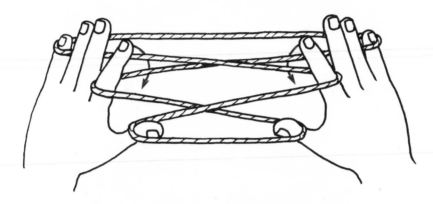

4. Let the index loops slide down on your index fingers until they are also held in the hooks of your index fingers.

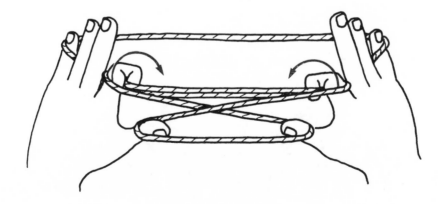

5. Rotate your index fingers towards you as you straighten them up to return to the basic position. Don't let your index fingers get tangled in the thumb loops.

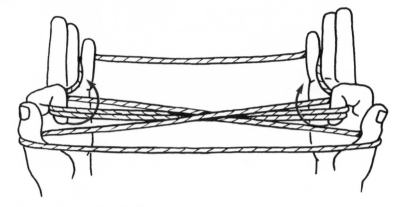

6. On each hand, there is a straight string which runs across the base of your fingers from index finger to little finger. Your thumbs, carrying their loops, go under the index loops to get these straight strings and return under the index loops to the basic position.

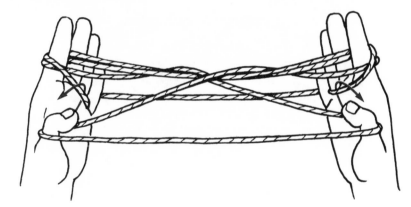

7. Each thumb now has two loops. Tip down your thumbs, or use your fingers or teeth, to Navaho the thumb loops.

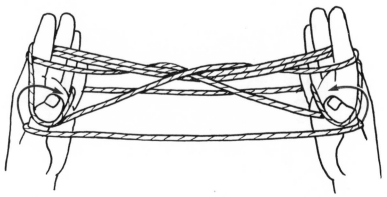

Keep going . . .

8. Your little fingers drop their loops. There is now a string X where the strings cross in the middle of the figure.

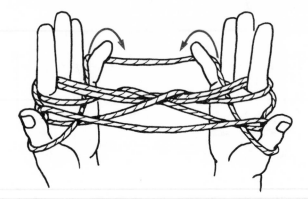

9. Turn your hands so that the palms are facing up. Your little fingers stretch to reach up, from below, into the top triangle of the string cross and hook down over the diagonal strings which make the cross. Return your hands to the basic position, but continue to hold the little finger loops in the hooks of your little fingers.

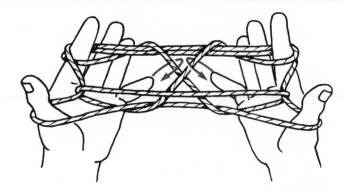

10. There is a straight string which runs across the figure from thumb loop to thumb loop. Grab this string with your teeth and hang on to it while your index fingers drop both their loops. Use your thumbs to help push these loops off your index fingers.

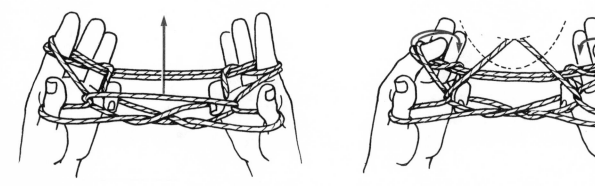

11. Now pull on the string you are holding between your teeth until the loose strings in the centre of the figure tighten, leaving only long little finger and thumb loops.

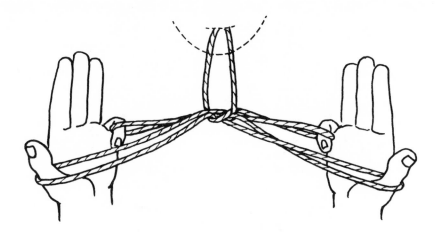

12. Release the mouth string, and Maui's Lasso will appear in the centre of the figure, looped around the strings. Turn your hands so that your fingers are pointing away from you. Now the Lasso is the right way up. Don't pull your hands apart unless you want your lasso to shrink!

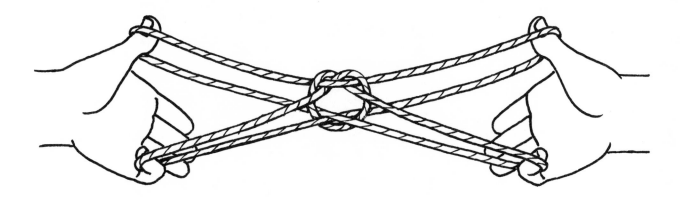

The Laia Flower

This string figure came from the New Hebrides. It's been called the Laia Flower and the Lotus Flower, and is one of a few truly three dimensional figures.

1. Do Opening A.

2. Turn your hands away from you a little and put all your fingers, including your little fingers, but not your thumbs, down into the little finger loops.

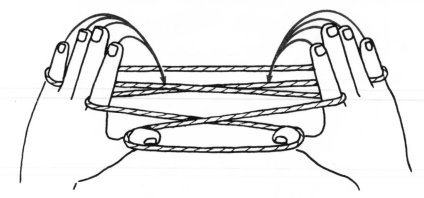

3. Throw these little finger loops around the backs of your ring, middle, and index fingers and straighten them up. Your little fingers have lost their loops. Keep these three-finger loops above the index loops and make sure that your thumbs have not sneaked into them as well.

4. Now put your thumbs and little fingers up into these three-finger loops and let these loops slide down around your wrists. You now have thumb loops, index loops, and wrist loops.

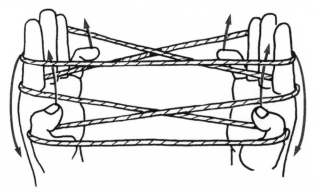

5. Bring your right little finger towards you under both strings of the right wrist loop. Your little finger pushes up these strings to get them out of the way, then hooks down over the right near thumb string. Your right little finger carries this string on its back as you return your hands to the basic position.

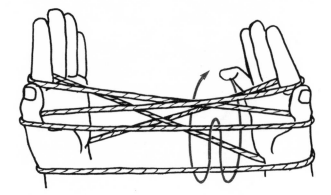

You now have a new right little finger loop.

6. Share this new right little finger loop with your left little finger by putting your left little finger up into the right little finger loop from below. Return your hands to the basic position.

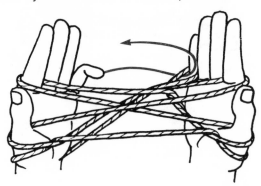

7. Transfer the index loops to your thumbs by putting your thumbs up into the index loops. Now take your index fingers out of their loops.

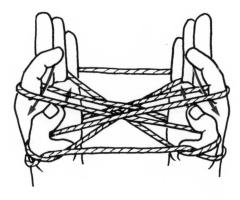

Keep going . . .

8. Your thumbs get the near little finger strings and return.

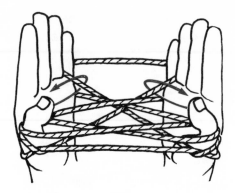

9. Your index fingers tip down and go up into the thumb loops to get the double far thumb strings and return.

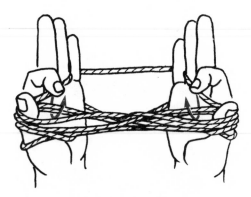

10. Your little fingers drop their loops.

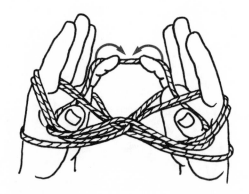

11. Your little fingers get the lower far index strings and return. As you get them, check that these strings cross over each other in the middle of the figure.

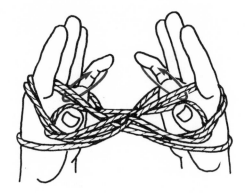

12. Your thumbs drop all their loops.

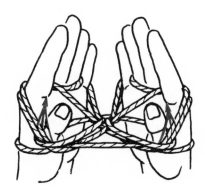

13. Turn your hands so that your fingers are pointing away from you and your thumbs are pointing up. There's the Laia Flower.

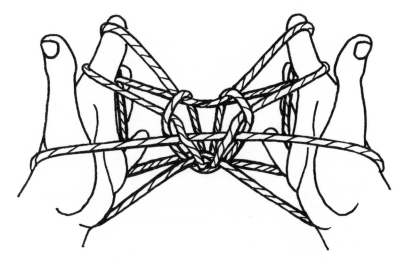

The King Fish

This string figure is about going fishing and about catching a thief. It comes from the Torres Straits in the South Pacific.

1. Do Opening A. Be sure to pick up with your right index finger first.

2. Your right index finger drops its loop. Pull your hands apart to tighten the strings.

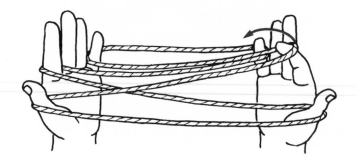

3. Your left index finger hooks down over the new left palmar string.

4. Your left thumb and little finger drop their loops. Your left index loop slides off your left index as this finger pulls out the loop it is holding in its hook. Once again, pull the strings until they are taut.

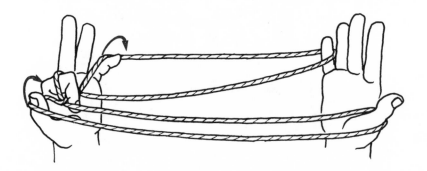

5. Your left thumb and little finger go up into the index loop from below to put this loop back on your left hand in Position 1. As you do this, take your left index finger out of its loop.

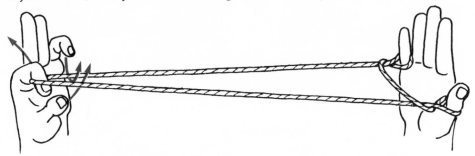

6. Your left index finger hooks down over the right palmar string. Rotate this finger towards you and up as you return to the basic position carrying a new twisted loop on your left index finger.

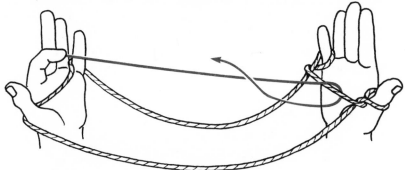

7. Your right index finger goes down, from the top, into the right thumb loop.

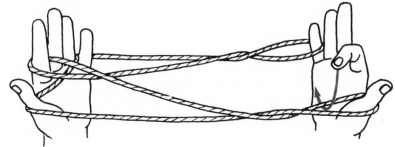

8. Your right index finger carries the far thumb string over with it as it then goes down into the right little finger loop.

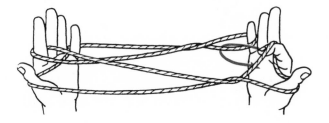

9. Your right index finger carries the near little finger string with it as it moves towards you and straightens up. This string becomes the new index loop.

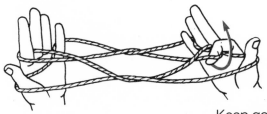

Keep going . . .

10. There is a string which crosses the right index loop. It is actually the right far thumb string. Your right little finger goes up into the right index loop and hooks down over this string. Don't worry about the right little finger loop. It can just slide off your right little finger.

11. At the same time, your left little finger hooks down the left far index string. Don't worry about the left little finger loop. It can just slide off your left little finger.

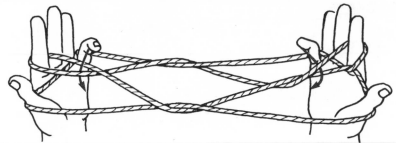

12. Keep the index loops high up on your index fingers and release your thumbs to extend the King Fish. You may have to adjust the strings slightly if the central diamond does not appear. You can usually reach over with your right thumb to do this.

Now comes the catchy part:
Ask a friend to put his/her hand into the central diamond of the figure. Will you catch the fish or not?
If you release your right hand and pull to the left, the fish will go free.
If you release your left hand and pull to the right, the fish will be caught in the net.
If you are very adept, you can do the whole figure backwards. (Pick up first with your left index. Drop your left index, etc.). Then, of course, when you release your right hand and pull to the left, the fish will be caught and vice versa.

This figure is also called Kamo, the thief.
A person is asked to put his/her hands into the central diamond and try to escape, either to the right or to the left. S/he will find that one end is closed and the other is open. If s/he goes to the closed side, s/he is Kamo, but if s/he goes to the open end, s/he is an honest person.

Many Stars

Sky things appear often in Navaho Indian string figures: lightning, storm clouds, and, of course, stars. On a clear night in the Arizona desert, there must indeed have been many stars.

1. Do Opening A.

2. Your thumbs go over the strings of the index loops to get the near little finger strings and return.

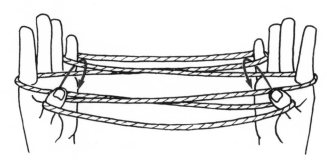

3. Your middle fingers go over the strings of the index loops to get the far thumb strings and return.

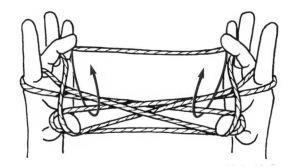

4. Your thumbs drop all their loops.

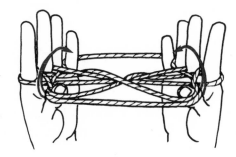

5. Your thumbs hook down the near index strings. Turn your hands so that the palms are facing out, and go under all the strings to get the far little finger string. Your thumbs bring this string out through the index loops. Return to the basic position.

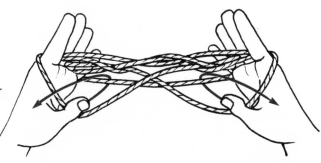

Keep going . . .

6. Your little fingers drop their loops.

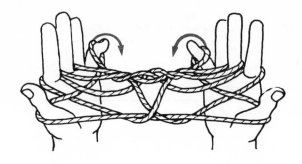

7. Move the middle finger loops up near the tops of your middle fingers. Turn your hands away from you a little and tip down your middle fingers so that you can see the far middle finger strings clearly. Now your index fingers can get the far middle finger strings and return.

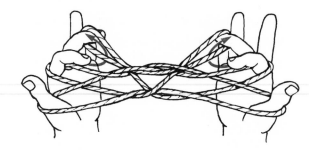

8. Your middle fingers drop their loops.

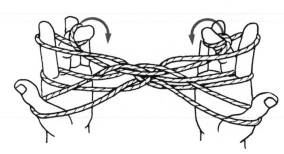

9. Your thumbs go up into the upper index loops and return. You've shared the upper index loops with your thumbs. Your thumbs and index fingers have lower single loops, and each thumb and index share a large upper loop. The large shared loops must stay above the lower single loops.

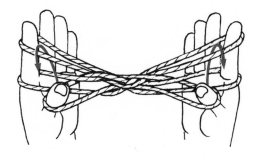

10. Now you want to Navaho the thumb loops. Use your fingers or teeth to bring the lower single right thumb loop and the lower single left thumb loop up over the large shared loop and over your right and left thumbs.

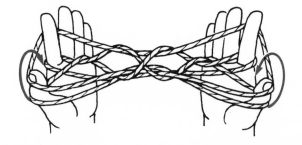

11. Now you want to Navaho the index loops. Use your fingers to bring the lower single right index loop and the lower single left index loop up over the shared loop and over your index fingers.

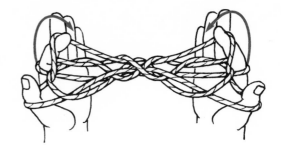

12. Now find the strings that go across the top of the thumb loops. Put your middle fingers, from below, up into the spaces on the far side of these strings. Hook your middle fingers down over these strings and down into the thumb loops.

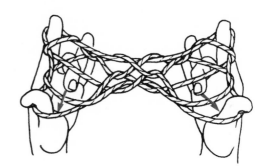

13. To get a nicely extended Many Stars, slide the index loops up near the tips of your index fingers. Your thumbs drop their loops to make Many Stars.

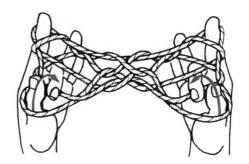

Here's a Navaho Indian story about the origin of string figures.

According to Navaho Indian legend, string games were taught to the Navaho by the holy spider people who were also human beings. The spider people taught the Navaho how to make various string figures of stars and coyotes, butterflies, and snakes. However, this game of string figures was to be played only in the winter, when spiders, snakes, and other animals sleep and so cannot see themselves imitated in string.

Why do you think the Navaho said that string games came from the spider people? Does the figure Many Stars remind you of a spider's web?

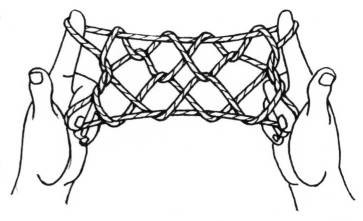

The Rabbit

This figure was collected in the early 1900s from a Klamath Indian named Emma Jackson who came from Oregon. It's another wonderfully realistic string picture.

1. Do Opening A.

2. Your index fingers tip down and go, from below, up into the thumb loops. Return to the basic position.

3. Your thumbs drop their loops.
   Each index finger now has two loops and there are loops on your little fingers. Be sure to keep the upper and lower index loops as far apart as you can.

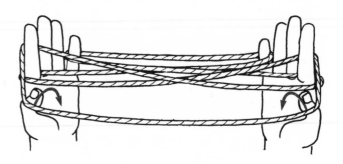

4. Turn your hands so that the fingers are pointing away from you and the thumbs are pointing up. Now there is a top string (the upper near index string), a bottom string (the far little finger string), and two string crosses in between.

5. Your thumbs are going to bring forward both the string crosses. So your thumbs go, from below, up into the little finger loops, then bring forward on their backs the near little finger strings, both strings of the lower index loops, and the far strings of the upper index loops.
   Return your hands to the basic position.

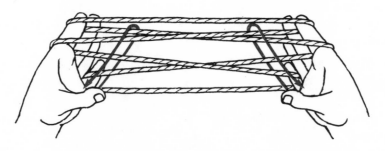

Be sure to keep the strings taut through the next manoeuvres.

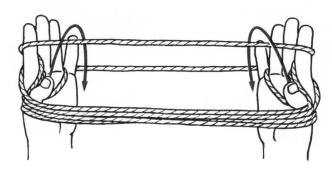

6. Now your thumbs hook down over the upper near index string. Don't worry about the strings on the backs of your thumbs. They'll just slide off.

7. Turn your hands so that the palms are facing out. Your thumbs, still carrying the upper near index string, go to get the far little finger string. Catch this string on the backs of your thumbs and bring it out under all the strings (except the one that was in the hook of your thumb).

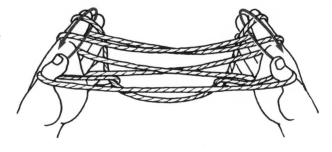

8. Stuff your thumbs up into the upper index loops. These are the small twisted index loops. If they are not on top, move them up.

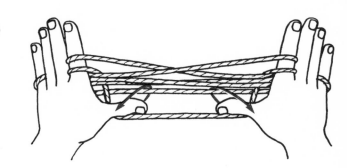

9. Navaho the thumb loops.

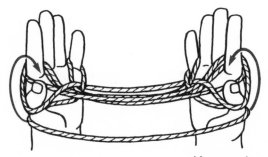

Keep going . . .

10. Use your right thumb and index finger to take off the upper left index loop and let it lie in the middle of the figure.

11. Use your left thumb and index finger to take off the upper right index loop and let it lie in the middle of the figure.

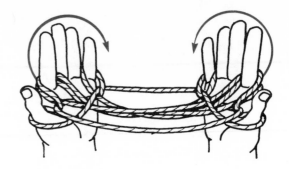

12. Your little fingers drop their loops. Don't pull the strings tight.

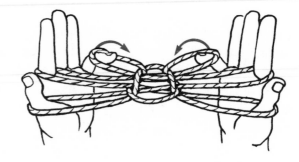

13. All your fingers come towards you across the strings and go down into the thumb loops.

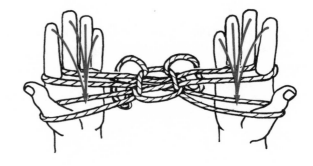

14. Your index fingers tip down to get the near thumb string, and then straighten up, carrying this string on their backs.

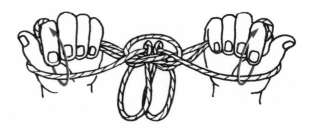

15. Your thumbs slide out of their loops.

16. Now use your thumbs to push the circular rabbit face away from you over his ears. His ears, looped over the far index string, will pop up. You may have to arrange the rabbit's face with your thumbs to make it symmetrical.

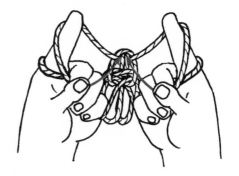

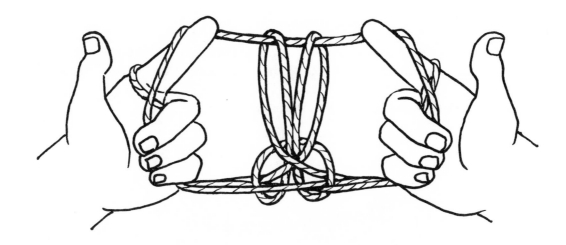

The Seagull or Man Carrying a Kayak

Some people say that this Inuit figure is a Seagull, but others say that it is a man carrying a kayak on his back. You can just see the legs of the man sticking out from underneath the large kayak. The movements of this figure are so fluid that the making of it is as much fun as the end result.

Keep all the strings as tight as you can while you make this figure and pay attention to the hand positions; they will help you find the strings you need.

1. Do Opening A.

2. Turn your hands so that the palms are facing away from you, and hook your index fingers down over the far index strings and both strings of the little finger loops.

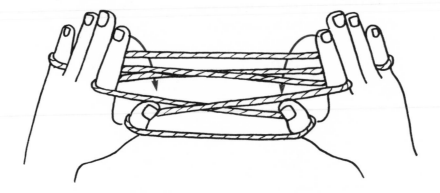

3. Your index fingers pull all these strings towards you and then they turn up into the thumb loops. Now you're in position for the next step. Don't worry about the index loops. They won't go anywhere.

4. With the sides of your index fingers, hook down the near thumb string.

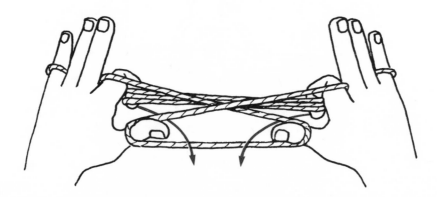

5. Now turn your index fingers away from you and up to return your hands to the basic position. As you do this, release the loops from your thumbs.

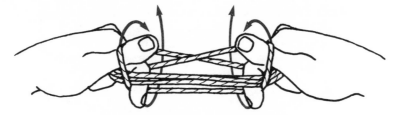

Each index finger now has an upper and lower loop (be sure to keep them separate) and each little finger has a loop.

6. Hook your thumbs over the lower near index strings and pull them down as far as you can. As you hook down the strings, turn your hands so that the palms are facing out and the thumbs are tilted down.

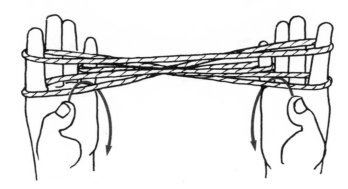

7. Your thumbs get the straight far little finger string. Now return your hands to the basic position. Don't worry about the old thumb loops. They'll just slip off your thumbs.

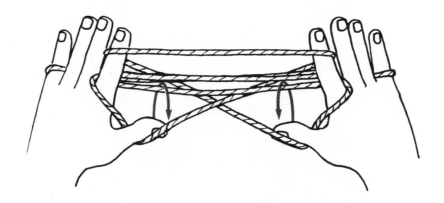

Keep going . . .

8. Your thumbs hook over the upper near index string and pull it down as far as they can. As you do this, let the new thumb loops slip off your thumbs.

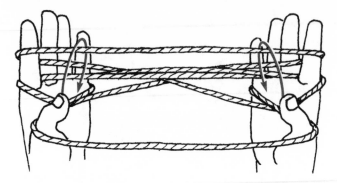

9. Turn your hands so that the fingers are pointing away from you. The near little finger strings run diagonally up to the centre of the figure. The far little finger strings run across your palms. Put your thumbs right into the triangular spaces created by these near and far little finger strings. Make sure your thumbs are near the centre of the figure.

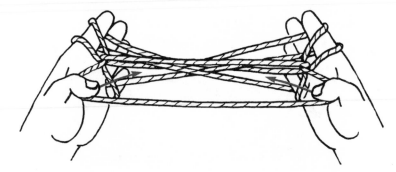

10. Turn your hands palms out again, thumbs down. Remember to keep the string taut.
Each thumb is holding down two strings: one straight string that runs from thumb to thumb, and one string that runs up diagonally towards the centre of the figure. These strings make a triangle in the centre of the figure. Are you still with me?
The backs of your thumbs bring forward, towards you, the strings that make the sides of the triangle. Let the straight thumb string slide off.

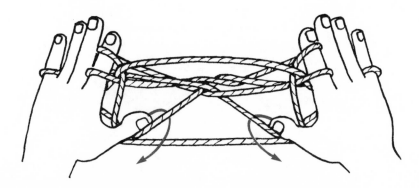

11. Move your hands sideways a little so that the tips of your fingers are closer; your thumbs can then point down. Your palms are still facing out.

12. Each thumb is holding down part of a string triangle. The base of each triangle is a straight string that runs across the figure. Your thumbs get that straight string and pull it towards you. The old thumb loops will just slip off your thumbs. Now return your hands to the basic position.

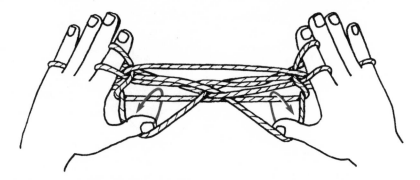

13. Each index finger has two loops. Use your right thumb and index finger to lift these loops right off your left index finger. Use your left thumb and index finger to lift these loops off your right index finger. Let all the index loops lie in the centre of the figure. You can tip your index fingers down into their loops, then down under the far index strings and up to do this more smoothly.

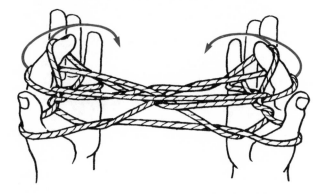

14. Turn your hands so that the fingers are pointing away from you and stretch your thumbs until they are pointing up. Now pull your hands gently apart until you can see the Seagull.

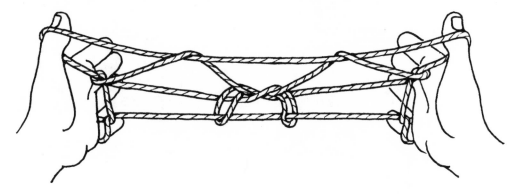

The Salt Cave

This figure comes from Hawaii. The chant that goes with it teaches a lesson about visitors and hospitality. It's a variation on the Fishnet, so it will be very easy to do if you already know that figure.

1. Do Opening A.

2. Turn your hands so that the palms are facing you and put all your fingers down into the thumb loops.

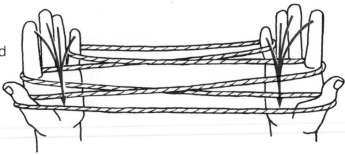

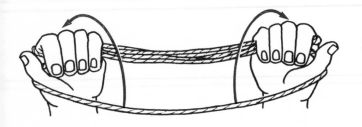

3. Throw the thumb loops over the backs of your hands and return your hands to the basic position. Be sure to keep all the loops separate. The loops around the backs of your hands should be lower than the index loops and the little finger loops.

4. Your thumbs go under the near strings of the hand loops to get the far little finger string. Return under the near strings of the hand loops.
   From now on, don't pay any attention to the hand loops.

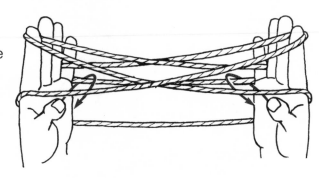

5. Your thumbs go over the near index strings to get the far index strings and return.

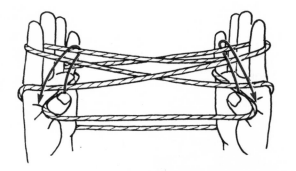

6. Your little fingers drop their loops.

62

7. Your little fingers go over the near index strings to get the far thumb strings and return.

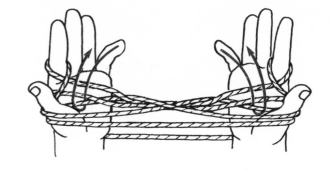

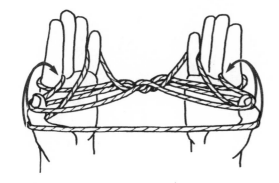

8. Your thumbs drop their loops.

9. Your thumbs go over the strings of the index loops to get the near little finger strings and return.

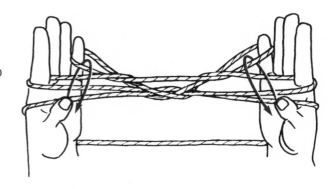

10. Use your right thumb and index finger to pull out the left index loop *and* the near string of the left hand loop. Share these loops with your left thumb.

11. Use your left thumb and index finger to pull out the right index loop *and* the near string of the right hand loop. Share these loops with your right thumb.

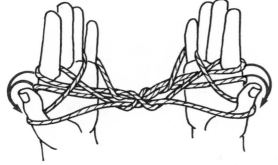

12. Tip down your thumbs, or use your fingers or teeth, to Navaho the thumb loops. The lowest thumb loop (it's not the hand loop!) goes up over the two other thumb loops and over the top of your thumb. After you've Navahoed, each thumb will still have two loops.

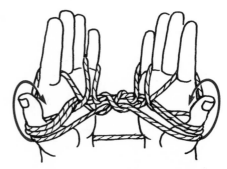

Keep going . . .

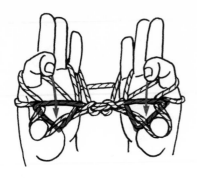

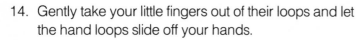

13. Near each thumb there is a string triangle. Your index fingers go down into these triangles.

14. Gently take your little fingers out of their loops and let the hand loops slide off your hands.

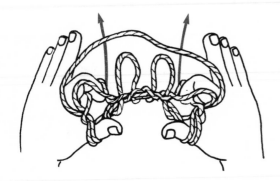

15. Turn your hands so that the palms are facing away from you.

16. Your index fingers straighten up to extend the net. Don't worry about the index loops; they will just slip off your index fingers. You now have the fishnet with one large free loop hanging loosely in front of it.

Try to avoid pulling and tugging the figure as you do steps 17, 18, and 19.

17. Turn your hands so that the palms face you, with your fingers almost meeting and your thumbs apart.

18. Your little fingers reach, from below, up into the thumb loops.

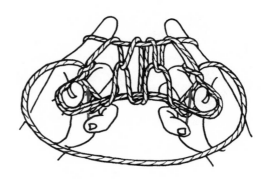

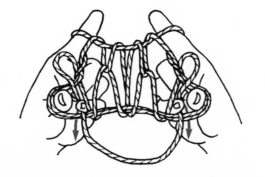

19. Use your mouth to grab the large free string loop and bring it across the thumb loops so that your little fingers can hook over the strings of this loop and draw them back out through the thumb loops. As you do this, let go of the string in your teeth.

20. Release the thumb loops to make the cave. Don't worry if your diamonds are flat the first few times. With a little practice and less tugging, they'll get better.

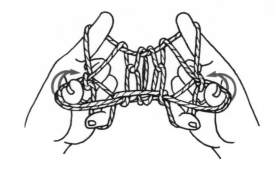

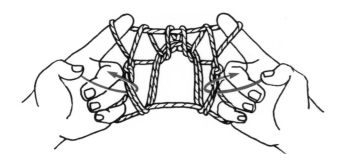

To close the doorway, your thumbs pull out the double strings that cross the little finger loops (these are the old thumb loops). To open the doorway, release these thumb loops.

Here's a story. Get ready to open and close the door at the right moments.

The setting is an ancient cave in the district of Kau on the island of Hawaii. Two men live in the cave. The chant that goes with the figure is the conversation between the man inside the cave and his servant outside who is guarding the door.

"A man, a man."
"Where is he?"
"Right here."
"What is in his hand?"
"No bundle of salt."
"Then shut, shut the door of our house."

Someone else appears and the conversation is repeated. This time, the answer is:
"A bundle of salt."

And the reply:
"Then open, open the door of our house."

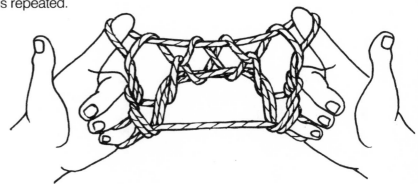

Solo Cat's Cradle (All By Yourself)

Solo Cat's cradle is played in Japan and Hawaii. You can experiment with having a friend step in to play along the way. Because of the way the strings cross over each other, sometimes you can turn it into a two-person game and sometimes you can't.

There are eight figures in the series — the eighth takes you back to the beginning again. Don't try to learn them all at once. It can be very frustrating, because if you make a mistake in the middle of figure 6, for example, you have to begin again from the first figure, Cradle. It's best to learn a couple of steps really well, and when you know those, build on them by adding a couple more until you can do them all.

And don't give up too easily. Your fingers can learn Solo Cat's Cradle. It's very impressive!

1. The Cradle

1. Do Opening A, picking up the palmar strings with your middle fingers.

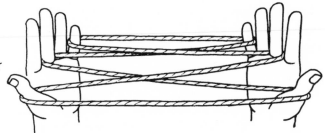

2. Cradle to Soldier's Bed

1. Turn your hands so that the palms are facing you. Put all your fingers down into the thumb loops and throw the thumb loops over the backs of your hands. The hand loops should be lower than the middle finger and little finger loops.

2. Turn your hands so that the palms are facing away from you. Put all your fingers, including your little fingers, but not your thumbs, down into the little finger loops and throw the little finger loops towards you over your fingers *and* your thumbs.

   You now have loops on your middle fingers and the hand loops cross over on the backs of your hands.

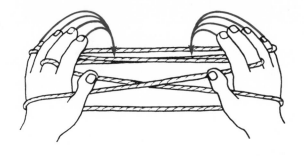

3. Your thumbs get the near middle finger strings.

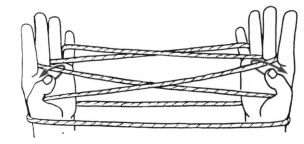

4. Your middle fingers drop their loops.

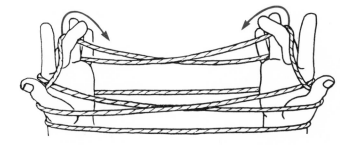

5. Tip your ring fingers and middle fingers down under the strings that lie between your ring fingers and little fingers. Let these strings slide over the backs of these fingers to lie in the space between your index fingers and middle fingers.

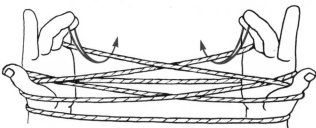

6. Tip your little, ring, and middle fingers down under the far string of the hand loops. Let this string slide over the backs of these fingers to also lie in the space between your middle fingers and index fingers. This is the Soldier's Bed.

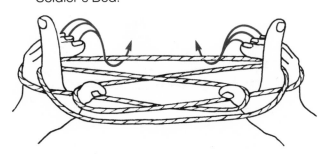

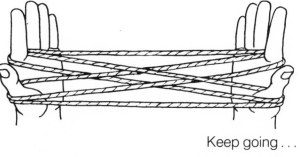

Keep going . . .

3. Soldier's Bed to Candles

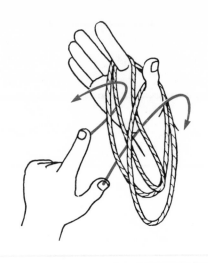

1. Take your left hand out of its loops.

2. Put your left thumb back up into the thumb loops from below, near your right thumb.

3. Put your left index finger back up into the index loops, from below, near your right index finger.

4. When you separate your hands to return to the basic position, you will see that the crosses have come undone — giving you Candles.

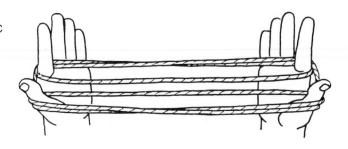

4. Candles to Diamonds

1. Your little fingers come towards you, over the strings, to get the far thumb candle string and return.

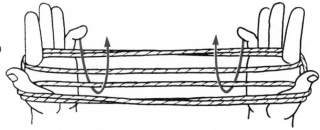

2. Your thumbs drop their loops.

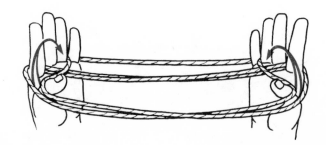

3. Look for the near straight string that runs from index finger to index finger. Your thumbs go under this string, then over all the strings of the index loops to get the near little finger strings and return. Each thumb now has two loops.

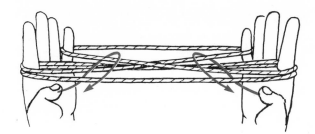

4. Your little fingers drop their loops.

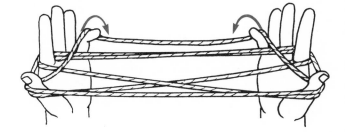

5. Hook your index fingers down, towards you, over the near index strings and keep these strings in the hooks of your index fingers while you let the other loops slide off your index fingers.

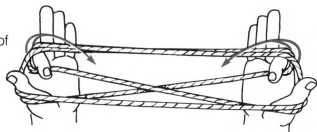

6. Straighten up your index fingers without twisting the index loops. There's now one loop on each index finger. (What a tidy Navaho!)

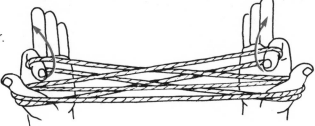

7. Look for the straight far thumb string which runs from thumb to thumb. Your index fingers tip down to get this string and return to make Diamonds.

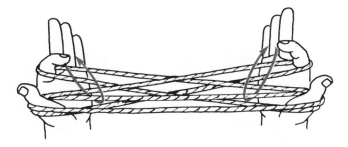
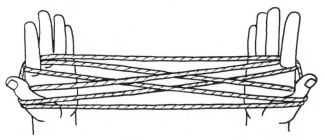

Keep going . . .

5. Diamonds to Cat's Eye

1. Your little fingers go up into the index loops.

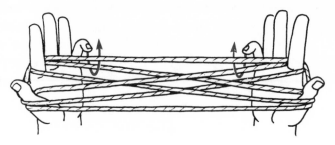

2. Your little fingers bring, on their backs, the crossed far index strings out under the straight far index string.

3. Your little fingers now go over the strings of the index loops to get the far thumb strings and return.

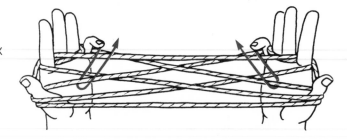

4. Your thumbs drop their loops to make Cat's Eye.

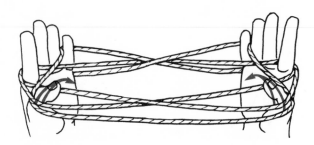 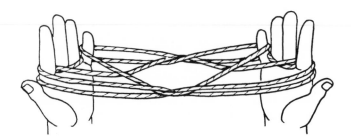

6. Cat's Eye to Drum or Scraggly

1. Your thumbs go up into the little finger loops. Move your thumbs towards each other until they can catch, on their backs, the diagonal strings which run from your index fingers to lace through the far little finger strings. Your thumbs return under the other strings to their usual position, carrying these strings with them as new thumb loops.

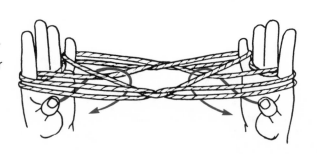

2. Your index fingers now hook down over the straight near little finger string. As they return to their usual position, the old double index loops will slip off your index fingers and this straight string will curve around your index fingers to become the far string of the new index loops.

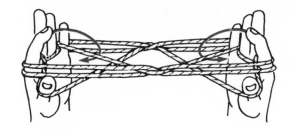

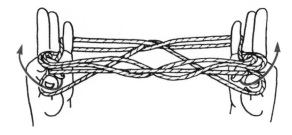

If you are standing up, please sit down, because you need a lap for the next step.

3. Each little finger has two loops: one ordinary loop, with a near and a far string; and one loop whose near string crosses your palm. Turn your hands so that the fingers are facing down, nearly touching your lap. Gently take your little fingers out of their double loops. When you release them, the near little finger strings that crossed your palm will become near index strings, leaving the other ordinary little finger loops lying on your lap.

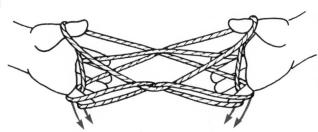

4. Use your little fingers like hooks to catch, from below, and hold, these little finger loops. Return your hands to the basic position. This is the Drum or Scraggly.

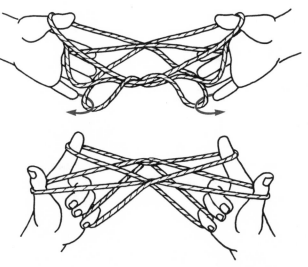

Keep going . . .

7. Drum to Manger

You have loops on your index fingers, loops on your thumbs, and loops held in the hooks of your little fingers.

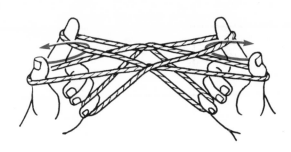

1. Your thumbs get the near index strings and return. You have shared the index loops with your thumbs.

2. Your index fingers, without losing their loops, get the far thumb strings, to share the thumb loops with your index fingers.

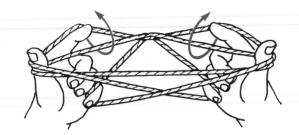

This is the Manger.

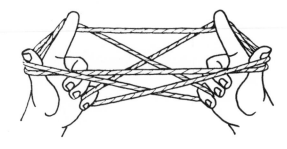

8. Manger to Cradle

Now you are elegantly going to return to the beginning so that, if you wish, you can start all over again.

1. So put your middle, ring, and little fingers, with their loops, up into the large shared thumb/index loops and let these loops slide down around your wrists. You now have double wrist loops and little finger loops.

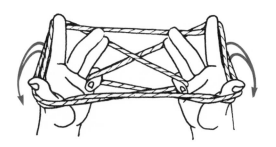

2. Your thumbs get the near little finger strings.

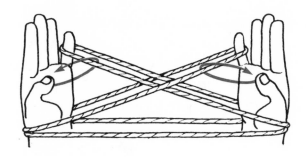

3. Do Opening A with your middle fingers.

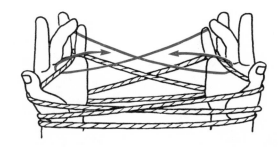

4. Now press the fingers of each hand tightly together so that the thumb, middle finger, and little finger loops do not slip off. Put your hands palm to palm and turn your fingers down to let the wrist loops slide off your wrists and hands.

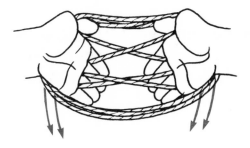

5. When you separate your hands and return them to the basic position, you will be back where you started, ready for applause, or ready to start all over again.

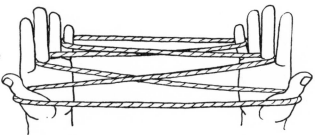

Stories in String

All over the world, string figures have been used to pass on histories and traditions from one generation to the next. These stories often told about the heroic deeds of demigods. These super heroes were part man and part god and were capable of super-human feats of courage and daring. Sometimes a performer would chant a story in a special way while making a string figure.

Some string figures, like **Maui's Lasso**, **The Salt Cave**, **The Land Crab,** and **The King Fish**, have their own stories. In Hawaii, a storyteller made a string figure and asked different members of the audience to identify it. The person who guessed correctly then chanted the song that went with the figure.

String figures and the stories of any people reflect the world around them. You could illustrate almost any story you know with your string. Remember there are no rules against making up stories, or even making up string figures, so use your imagination.

It take a little practice to be able to talk while your fingers are flying. You have to know the figures so well that you can do them without thinking. You also have to learn to pace your story so that your fingers can keep up.

The Reluctant Sun, **Maui's Lasso**, and **Maui and the Mud Hens** will give you an idea of how stories and string figures go together. If you know other string figures, you can always embroider a story to include them.

The Reluctant Sun

Here's the story of some "sunny" string magic from the
Gilbert Islands in the South Pacific. It's built around a figure
that looks very much like the **African Moon** (see p. 29),
so you can use this figure when you tell the story.

Once upon a time, a long time ago in the South Pacific,
people noticed that the sun was having difficulty setting
each evening. As the day came to its end, the sun would
begin to go down in the usual way, sinking towards the
place where the sky and the sea meet. Then, suddenly,
it would seem to change its mind. As if it were afraid of
something, it would struggle to climb higher in the sky
before giving up and finally disappearing below the
horizon.

People began to worry that the sun might decide not to set
at all. It would always be day. Nobody would be able to
sleep. The night creatures would never get up. And most
of all, there would be no more beautiful sunsets. So they
decided to use the magic in string figures to help the
sun set.

One evening, a group of people went to a beach on the
western side of their island in order to be as near to the sun
as possible. Then one of them made the string figure the sun
(**African Moon**), and held it out at arm's length towards the
real sun. Together they chanted, "Tiroron, tiroron, tiroron,
tiroron," which meant, "Roll, roll, roll, roll. Roll down your
path in the sky." Then, to encourage the sun to hurry up,
they reminded it that dinner was waiting: "Below you is your
food, the shark."

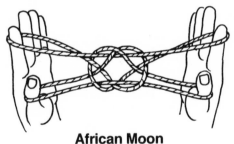

African Moon

As they chanted, the person who had made the sun figure
slowly pulled his hands apart and the string figure became a
knot. Everybody cried, "The sun sets!" The string magic
had worked.

On many other evenings, people in the Gilbert Islands
gathered on a western beach and performed this string
ritual to help the reluctant sun on its way.

Maui's Lasso

After Maui had lifted the heavens away from the earth, there was room for the sun to come up from the lower world and run across the blue vault of the sky. The sun was strong and full of energy, and made his journey so quickly that the days were hot and very short.

Maui's mother, Hina, complained to her son. "How can our people get all their work done if the days are so short? We pound the wood pulp for our kapa cloth, but by the time we spread it out to be dried by the sun, he has already rushed across the sky, and we have to gather it up and wait for the next day. We don't even have enough time to prepare and cook our food in one day. Everyone is grumbling about the sun."

Maui saw how discouraged his people were, and how much trouble the thoughtless sun caused. He agreed to speak to the sun, and threaten him if necessary, until the sun promised to go more slowly across the sky.

Early one morning, before dawn, he took his **lasso** and climbed to the top of Mount Haleakala, the mountain called the House-of-the-sun.

As the sun climbed out of the pit of night, Maui got his lasso ready to catch him, but he only caught one of the sun's long rays and broke this leg off. He threw his lasso again, and broke off another of the sun's strong legs.

Maui's Lasso

At last, after Maui had thrown his lasso many times, he caught the sun and threatened to punish him for going so quickly. But the sun begged and pleaded for his freedom.

"If you will release me, I promise to go more slowly. You have broken off all my strong legs and left me with only my little weak legs to carry me on my journey across the sky."

So Maui let the sun go. And the sun kept his promise. From that day, he travelled more slowly so that Maui's mother, and all of Maui's people, had time to finish their day's work.

Maui and the Mud Hens

The **Reluctant Sun** and **Maui's Lasso** illustrate a single string figure. This story is much longer, and you have to make many figures as you tell it!

Maui was also responsible for bringing the secret of fire-making to his people. Here's one way that Maui is said to have tricked the keepers of the fire.

Hina, Maui's mother, wanted some fish (**King Fish**). Early one morning, Maui and his three brothers, seeing that the storm waves of the sea had died down, left their house and set out for the good fishing grounds.

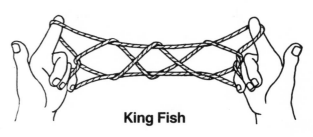

King Fish

As Maui and his brothers walked down to their canoe on the beach, they saw seagulls (**Seagull**) circling over the water.

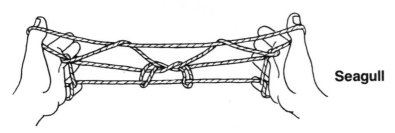

Seagull

Maui and his brothers got into their canoe (**Well or Dugout Canoe**) and paddled away from shore. When they got to the good fishing grounds, they threw out their nets (**Many Stars**) and began to fish.

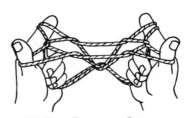

Well or **Dugout Canoe**

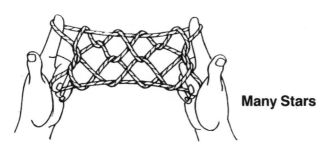

Many Stars

As they were fishing, Maui looked towards the land, towards the mountains (**Two Bears and Their Caves**), and saw smoke curling up into the sky.

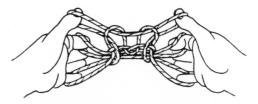

Two Bears and Their Caves

Now Maui's people had been without fire for many years since the great volcano Haleakala had become extinct. Try as they might, they had been unable to keep their last coals alive. They lived on fruits, uncooked roots, clams (**Giant Clam**) and eels (**Eel**), and other fish raw from the sea. But now, Maui hoped to get fire, and cooked food once more.

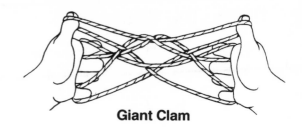

Giant Clam

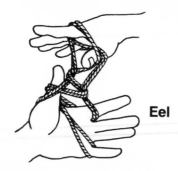

Eel

"There's a fire (**Fire**) burning," he cried. "Let's go right away and see whose it is." But after some talk, he and his brothers decided that first they should catch some fish before the hot sun drove them deep into the cool sea. Then, they would have something to cook.

So they fished until the bottom of their boat was covered with their catch, then they beached their canoe. Maui's brothers returned to their task and Maui set off to find the source of the smoke.

Meanwhile, up on the mountainside, two brother Alae, or Curly Tailed Mud Hens, were cooking their favourite food, baked bananas. But as they were cooking, they were watching, and when they saw only three brothers in the boat, they knew that the fourth was searching for them. When Maui reached them, they were already scratching out their fire (**Lochiel's Dogs or Chicken Toes**).

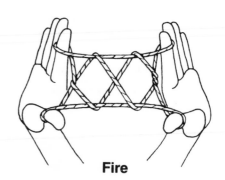

Fire

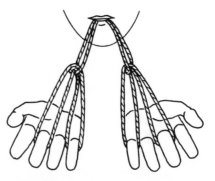

Lochiel's Dogs or **Chicken Toes**

And when their work was done, they flew away (**Open the Gate**).

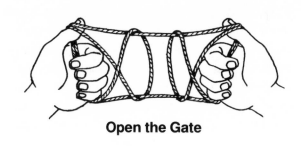

Open the Gate

Day after day, Maui and his brothers watched for smoke, but the Alae made no fire (**Fire**).

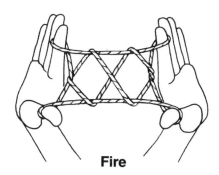

Fire

One day, Maui's brothers went fishing again and Maui stayed behind to watch. But again the mud hens saw only three brothers in the boat and said to each other, "Three are in the boat and we don't know where the other one is. We will make no fire (**Fire**) today."

Finally, Maui rolled up a piece of cloth and propped it up in his place in the boat. Then he followed the birds from secret place to secret place until he came to Waianae on the island Oahu. There he saw a great fire. A crowd of birds was chattering loudly and trying to hurry up the cooking bananas by chanting, "Let us cook quickly, Let us cook quickly. Maui, the swift child of Hina, will come."

Maui knew that the smallest mud hen, Alae-Iki, was the one who kept the secret of fire making, so he grabbed him, and shook him, demanding the fire secret.

The littlest mud hen, hoping to distract Maui and escape, told him that fire was made by rubbing together two bananas. Maui, seeing the bananas in the fire, thought that this was reasonable and began to rub together pieces of banana (**Fire** figure, not extended. Move hands back and forth to rub the strings together).

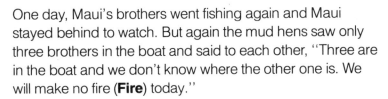

Fire figure, not extended

But the only result was banana juice, and Maui became very angry. Again he threatened the littlest mud hen, Alae-Iki. Alae-Iki told him that fire came from rubbing together water reeds, so Maui (as above) rubbed together two water reeds. Maui was watchful as well as angry, and he became angrier still when all he got for his efforts was water. Again he threatened the bird — and this time Alae-Iki told him that fire came from rubbing together (as above) green sticks. But the sticks were so green that they could give no fire. Now Maui became so angry and threatened Alae-Iki so fiercely that the little mud hen was afraid for his life and taught Maui how to make fire by rubbing together dry sticks from trees where fire lived (**Fire** figure, rub strings).

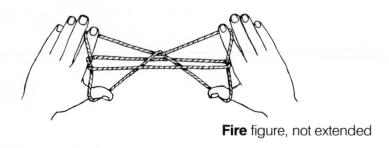

Fire figure, not extended

And Maui made fire (Extend **Fire**).

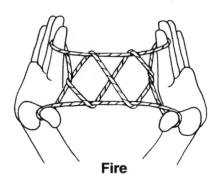

Fire

And this is how Maui's people learned how to draw out the sparks that lived in different kinds of trees.